I0468141

Welcome! Whether you are in class with me or reading this on your own, I am grateful for the opportunity to be of service to you. I created this workshop to help employees learn how to deal effectively with the impact bad workplaces are having on their lives. My goal is to give you new strategies for dealing with whatever nonsense you are facing at work, and help you get your life back. I have a completely different set of training resources to teach leaders how to be their best selves, how to build great teams for amazing results, and how to have an incredible, positive impact on their organizations and communities. For now though my focus is on you, the employee. Regardless of what position you hold in your organization, if you have someone above you, next to you, or under you who is robbing you of safety and health, what you'll learn today can make a vital and perhaps even life-saving difference.

Everyone deserves a safe, healthy, productive work environment. Yet too many of today's organizations aren't even thinking about safety or health as an organizational objective. Too many of today's leaders are untrained, dysfunctional, or otherwise compromised. Their personal issues invade the workplace and wreak havoc. They make it impossible to accomplish the mission. They cause problems that range from aggravating to dangerous.

Weak leaders also dump dealing with problems on their employees. They refuse to listen, live in complete denial, and cover up misconduct. They leave people to fend for themselves, without the ability or the authority to resolve problems. They send their best employees to workshops about how to deal with difficult people. They hire guest speakers to conduct what amounts to pep rallies to distract people from the reality of the problems they face. They do teambuilding activities just to give the appearance of caring. There is nothing authentic about those leaders, and they do not possess a good intent towards others. Their entire goal is to serve their own needs. They will manipulate people and engineer situations for their own advantage, at the expense of the team. Those types of leaders do massive damage to their employees' health, marriages, families, and lives. Those negative impacts rarely make the news, but they fundamentally alter the course of people's futures.

It is my firm belief that those leaders will be ultimately be held accountable for the damage they have caused. They are spiritually responsible for the impact they have on the people under their command. There will come a day when they will have all the hurt and destruction they forced upon their team come back to them. But until that day comes, we have to deal with them. The information I'm going to teach you systematically leads you through a comprehensive assessment of the problem and its impact on you, and then shifts into strategies for solving the problems and minimizing the impact. Even if you think your situation is so unique or so toxic that nothing at all can help, hang in there and keep working through these exercises. There is hope.

Section One: Assess the Problem

We can't possibly solve something we don't understand. Bad leaders create a lot of confusion about what is really going on in an organization. That dynamic is sometimes very deliberate. Some leaders operate in the shadows, making shady deals, telling lies, and pitting people against each other. If a leader can cause chaos among the troops, it diverts attention from anyone realizing that the root of the problem is the leader. This kind of work environment is exhausting and exasperating to deal with. Healthy people in these environments, who see the truth and speak up against the drama, often experience immense pressure to conform to the leader's warped spin on reality. They are made to feel abnormal for being healthy. The pressure can be so intense that people start doubting themselves, and wondering if they are wrong, or if they are the problem. This has a corrosive effect on the individual, the team, the organization, and the stakeholders. Stepping back from the dynamics is essential to recognizing where the problems are actually coming from.

Three Sources of Trouble in Organizations

Problems at work can be overwhelming. It helps to break them down into a more manageable size by figuring out where the issues are coming from. There are three sources of trouble at work: co-workers, leaders, or the system. We're going to take a look at them one by one. Later in the presentation, you'll have a chance to take a look at whether or not you are playing any kind of role in the problems, but for now we're going to talk about when the problem is someone else. The popular theory that both individuals in a conflict are always at fault is false. Sometimes issues really are the handiwork of just one person and those around them are victims of either circumstance or opportunity. Let's talk more about where problems originate from:

1. **Co-workers.** Our co-workers are a huge part of our lives. We spend significant time with them and their impact on us is inescapable. The best situations are those in which the problem individual is an anomaly in an otherwise healthy work environment. Examples include people who are impaired in some way, are facing overwhelming stress outside the office, have a poor work ethic, have a lack of personal accountability, or who have an entitlement mentality. Our best experiences are with people who are generally great to work with but who go through occasional rough patches. Our worst experiences are those in which our co-workers come to work unable or unwilling to do their part to create a healthy, productive work environment, and rob the rest of us from having that critically important foundation for a good work life. Dysfunctional people will cause disruption in the work environment to one degree or another.

2. **Leaders.** Impaired leaders destroy people, environments, and missions. Examples are somewhat similar to co-workers, but have a greater impact due to the power the leader holds over the workplace and everyone in it. Impaired leaders force their people to carry at least part of the leader's burdens. This derails the mission and generates immense resentment among healthy people who are stuck with extra duties as well as having to tend to the emotional wreckage left in the impaired leader's wake. If the leader becomes overwhelmed by stress outside the office, it will at a minimum temporarily throw them off their game. Leaders may also have a lack of skills for dealing with people, problems, or running high achieving teams. Even if a leader has never had the opportunity to attend college, there are still plenty of training options between in-house workshops, seminars in the community, or online classes. There are a lot of free options these days, and if all else fails, reading books or listening to books on CD as you commute each day is a great way to learn how to improve your leadership skills. Some leaders might not have a natural aptitude of leadership ability, but again this can be strengthened and learned through the training methods described above. Leadership also magnifies flaws. Leaders have to be mature enough to become their best selves and bring their A game to the workplace everyday. Without question, the most grave flaw a leader can have is the absence of a sound ethical foundation. If a leader does not have personal AND professional integrity, then the workplace doesn't stand a chance of real success. The good people on board may keep the organization from going completely under, and they may keep the team patched up enough to keep limping along for awhile, but eventually that workplace will implode under the weight of the leader's misdeeds. Either the good people will leave, legal actions will be filed, profits will precipitously decline, or organizational goals will not be met. Eventually, what has been wrong all along is exposed, and like a cockroach running out of a corner when a flashlight shines, the guilty parties have nowhere left to run and hide.

3. **The system.** Sometimes the problem is not difficult co-workers or leaders, but a system that is inherently predisposed to allow problems to arise and flourish. Examples include systems that greatly constrain or prohibit consequences for bad behavior, toxic cultures, good old boys (or girls) clubs, a hierarchy that diffuses accountability to the point of irrelevance, or control that lies outside the organization. If managers aren't allowed to discipline or fire people, the work environment will be greatly compromised. If the organization utilizes misconduct as a justified means to a profitable end, that is a systemic toxic culture. It won't matter how many good people are acting in good faith, their values and best efforts will not be supported by the company. If the system operates on power being reserved exclusively for those who are part of a select group that has their own

hidden agenda, instead of a common vision to fulfill the mission of the organization, no good person can overcome that either. If the organization is so top heavy that no one really knows who the decision makers are, it will be impossible to find the kind of accountability that facilitates problem resolution. If the organization is obligated to stakeholders on the outside, those individuals come into play as well. Even if every person in the company is doing their best, one flawed individual who holds any kind of power outside the organization can short-circuit efforts to solve problems. Corrupt people create corrupt systems, and they gleefully gorge at the trough of their largesse. Right up until the day the news cameras come calling, and accountability is inescapably visited upon them.

THE #1 QUESTION TO ANSWER WHEN YOU ARE FACED WITH A BAD WORK SITUATION

One of the most critical questions you can ask about your workplace gets right to the heart of the matter. Is the problem individual a person of essentially good character who occasionally makes mistakes? Or are they an essentially flawed character who occasionally manages not to mess things up? The answer to that question dictates your strategy.

If the issues are with someone who is essentially of good character, then there is a lot of hope for a complete resolution. Using your best interpersonal skills will go a long way towards resolving the issues. But if the person is of poor character, especially if they have a malicious or merciless intent towards other people, you are in a highly concerning situation because the only thing that matters to people like that is advancing their own agenda. They are willing to sacrifice you and everything that matters to you in pursuit of their own gain. Even the most advanced communication and conflict resolution skills do not work with them. Entirely different strategies are called for. Using healthy skills makes us more vulnerable to these individuals, because they exploit our personal honor code of treating people well and fairly. The sole goal with these people is to contain their behavior in such a way that it stops harming us.

 True resolution of problems with ill-intentioned people is not possible, because solving issues is not their point. The conflict itself is the point. These folks continually try to bait others into interactions they can use to their advantage. If you engage, you lose. These people do some of the worst damage to people's minds, hearts, and souls. They destroy trust in life and other people because they instigate tremendous amounts of conflict, then blame the other person for it. They toy with people for the sport of it and leave a lot of destruction in their wake.

For example, if your co-worker or leader has a good track record of treating people well, doing their own job to the best of their ability, and taking accountability for the occasional mistakes they do make, then there's a high likelihood they will genuinely try to resolve problems when they are brought to their attention. Conversely, your co-worker or leader may have a history of being a jerk to people, doing their own job marginally, not taking responsibility and blaming others for pretty much everything. But they may occasionally throw a pizza party so that they can say they did. With that kind of track record, that's not a person who is going to be interested in hearing about, let alone resolving, conflict. You have to look at what is most consistent about them over time.

If you have a generally good and trustworthy co-worker or leader, give them the benefit of the doubt and do your best to work with them to resolve anything that comes up. They'll appreciate your honesty even if it's hard for them to hear, because they have a demonstrated interest in having a healthy, productive workplace. If you have a co-worker or leader who typically acts disrespectfully and doesn't seem to care, then it's a mistake to think they will take whatever specific issue you are bringing up seriously. It will make you more vulnerable to more problems if you try to use healthy skills to work things out. It is not your responsibility to trust those who have proven they can't be trusted.

CATEGORIES OF TROUBLED CO-WORKERS / LEADERS

It's also essential to determine what type of impairment is compromising your co-worker's or leader's ability to function in a healthy way. Or at least take your best educated guess based on your observations of and experiences with the person. While problems will vary by degree and individual, there are five main categories of impairments:

1. **Addiction.** The individual may be addicted to a substance or activity. Or they may be involved in other people's addictions. Or they may have grown up in family that had an addict in it. Active addiction issues encroach on the work environment. The addict may be using their substance or engaging in their activity on the premises, at lunch, or on company time. Or they may keep the active use out of the workplace, but the effects still cause significant problems. Signs can include poor attendance, lack of productivity, being preoccupied to the point of distraction, mood swings based on getting their fix, hostile interactions with others, lying, cheating, stealing, secretive behavior, and punishment for those who do not help cover the addict's tracks.

In much the same way, people who grew up in an addicted family and who have never dealt with those issues also show classic behavioral traits that disrupt the work environment, often creating a toxic undercurrent that erodes trust, productivity, and mission accomplishment. It also does a lot of damage to healthy people, in much the same way that a daily dose of poison would hurt a healthy person. There are some great lists online about the behaviors that are commonly seen in adult children of addicted families. We don't have time to go into them in detail today, but in general it comes down to a person living by rigid rules and roles, with severe consequences for anyone who steps outside that restricted world. The goal with every trait, rule, and role is to protect the addict from the consequences of his/her own behavior. The addict shoves off their responsibility to the rest of the family, and rather than taking responsibility for themselves, they force their family to take the responsibility for them. It is crazy making for people who aren't actually responsible for something, to be required to take responsibility. There is a lot of hysteria about this. If someone doesn't play their part, the addicted family acts as if it is a matter of life or death. They will stop at nothing to make the healthy person look like the sick person. There is enormous desperation to hide the truth.

The addicted family creates a highly distorted world for everyone in it. It's not always clear to the people inside that system, what is real and what is distorted. When the children of these families grow up and enter the work force, if they have never dealt with these issues, they will end up functioning in their teams the way they functioned in their family. Leaders will end up creating workplaces that function like their addicted family. They will select a narrative for themselves, perhaps that they need to be taken care of (the victim). This translates to a mandate that their employees keep secrets for them so they don't face consequences for their behavior. If there is a staff member who grew up in an addicted family and never dealt with their issues either, they will leap to the defense of the leader at any cost (the rescuer). Healthy employees who have dealt with their issues and make good choices and don't buy into the sick rules or roles they are supposed to play are branded the enemy (the villains). What happens in these situations is a battle develops between the healthy people wanting to do their jobs, and the unhealthy people wanting to stage a drama each day. The "victims" send out distress signals to the "rescuers" and together they fight to vanquish the "villains". They replicate in the work environment what took place in their living room growing up. This causes mass damage to people and missions.

2. **Mental health.** The individual may have a psychological or emotional issue they are dealing with. This can range from an acute reaction to life stress, to full blown episodes

of mental illness. Signs can include erratic behavior, unpredictable moods, high levels of conflict with other people, or a loose grip on reality. It is important to distinguish between situational stress that exists due to an external challenge in only one environment, versus problematic behavior that is generated by the individual and is pervasive across environments.

We all face situational stress. Health problems, family issues, money troubles, or other types of difficulties can throw anyone temporarily off their game. It's possible to have more than one life problem at once, and be in a highly stressed state, but again it is temporary. The trouble is coming from the stressors overwhelming the coping skills or other resources the person has to resolve them. The pressure is coming from the outside of the person, and they are doing their best to adapt to it.

Mental health issues are internal. The pressure comes from inside the person and it shows up in how they deal with just about everything and everyone. They tend to experience the same kinds of problems in all their environments, including work, family and personal life. This is not to say they are bad people. It is important only in terms of trying to figure out how to deal with the impact on the work environment. If you are dealing with someone with a true mental illness, it may be that they aren't able to respond well to attempts to work towards more acceptable behavior. People under situational stress who are advised about the impact of their behavior/attitude on the team will generally pause and realize the problems are bleeding over into work. They will at least make a good faith effort to get themselves back on track well enough to function in the work environment. They are capable of seeing their behavior accurately, understanding its impact, and then making positive change. People with true mental illness however, may lack the capacity for that kind of insight, empathy, and behavioral adjustment. There is a lot of good information online about how specific disorders affect people, if you are interested in learning more about signs and symptoms. These people are typically wanting to do a good job, but have organic issues that makes it really tough for them.

3. **Criminal activity.** We can't pretend this doesn't happen just because it's an uncomfortable topic for some people to think about. We like to see the best in people, but it's necessary for us to face the harsh reality that some people make choices in their lives to become involved in illegal activities. Some of these people will engage in illegal behavior while at work. They may steal from the company, gain access to confidential information

and use it for personal gain, exploit customers, or even use their workplace as an operational outpost for their criminal enterprise. Even if people are involved in criminal activity only outside of work, the effects of that can still greatly impact the environment. Signs can include sudden unexplained improvement in socioeconomic status, secretive behavior, bragging about their exploits, co-workers witnessing suspicious transactions, or association with questionable people. These people will have zero interest in changing their behavior because they are profiting from it too much. All the advanced communication skills workshops in the world won't help when dealing with this kind of issue. These people don't honor the spirit or mission of a workplace, they corrode it. If they perceive someone as interfering with their activities, they can turn dangerous or even violent.

4. **Drama stagers.** For those of you who have not yet read the work of Dr. Alan Godwin, I highly recommend his book "How to Solve Your People Problems," (published 2011, dralangodwin.com) Dr. Godwin gives us the incredible gift of teaching us skills about how to deal with people who have a bad intent towards others, or who are simply so wrapped up in themselves they do not care what the impact of their behavior is on other people. His work fills in the missing piece for those of us who have sat through workshop after workshop on dealing with difficult people and then left saying "this doesn't work with the people I am dealing with." You can read Dr. Godwin's work for the details, but for now I am going to add my perspective on the conversation he so eloquently started.

Drama stagers create particularly crazy making environments. Their behavior differs from people who grew up in addicted families. When adult children learn the telltale signs of how their addicted family impacted them, their life suddenly makes sense in a brand new way. They are generally grateful for the information and strive to overcome the effects of the past. For them, there was always a sense of something not quite being right but never really being able to figure out what it was, or why life wasn't working for them. It is a relief to realize the problems can be fixed.

Drama stagers however, are well aware of their behavior and they coldly calculate using it to gain an advantage at the expense of those around them. They may have grown up in an addicted family, they may have grown up in a healthy family. They may have an addiction issue, they may not. They may or may not have mental health issues. Whatever their background is, the defining characteristic of these people is that they choose to continue acting in destructive ways because of the benefits it provides them. They can be merciless, and have no problem sacrificing other people and what is important to them. These folks have an inflexible narrative about themselves and the world. They will do anything to preserve, protect, and defend that narrative. They constantly scan for threats, challenges, or violations of their narrative.

Essentially, they have decided what their life should be like and assigned the rest of us roles that support their desired objective. We are almost always unaware of our role, but still get punished when we don't play our part. For example, someone may have a narrative that they are superior to everyone else. The role they have assigned themselves is to be the everlasting, brilliant star of any situation. The role they have assigned the rest of us is to be subservient. All of this goes largely undetected except for the uneasy gut feeling people get when they are around the drama stager. Until one day in a meeting, someone asks a question because they are seeking information, and the drama stager flips out because they think the person who asked the question is trying to make them look stupid. So they viciously verbally attack the person who asked the question. In their mind, the attack was justified because their rules were violated. But everyone else is horrified, and sees the attack as being wildly out of line. It is as crazy and convoluted as it sounds. It doesn't take more than one or two of these types of episodes before healthy people conclude something is really wrong with this type of individual, and start steering clear of them.

If you have more than one drama stager in the work environment, and their narratives serve one another's purposes, then you'll see even bigger and more chaotic scenes play out. In order to keep the drama going and keep everyone in an uproar so the focus is deflected from their own bad behavior, drama stagers attack people not problems. A lot of healthy people make the mistake of thinking that if they just solve whatever the drama stager is screaming about it will fix things and then there will be no more drama. But unfortunately that is a common scenario of the drama stager exploiting the healthy person's kindness or other values. Drama stagers don't want things to be fixed. They want their narrative to be reinforced. Spinning people in circles is the point. Actually fixing things is not. Drama stagers are weapons of mass disruption in the work environment, creating upheaval where there had been none before. These people use work to feed their own emotional needs, which bizarrely includes destroying people, places, and things. Work is a theater for them, a stage upon which their daily moods and whims can be acted out. Actually earning their paycheck and being a productive member of the work society is the furthest thing from their mind.

5. **Immaturity.** We all know people who simply have not grown up. Perhaps they are lacking in skills, or perhaps it is their choice. Regardless of the reason, they cause plenty of chaos in the workplace because they do not handle themselves in a mature, professional manner. There are lots of behavioral variations on this theme, but the core similarity is that these people are stuck in a developmental age very different from their chronological age.

These are the types of people who ridicule others. They bolster their own egos by making fun of pretty much everybody. They can be easily spotted, huddled up in the back of the room whenever a meeting is going on, laughing, poking each other, making faces, and otherwise showing off for each other. They can also be found in the lunchroom, gossiping, talking trash, and bullying their co-workers. I call this the arm-fart stage of development. It is behavior that is typically found at the junior high level. What these self-appointed cool kids fail to realize is that their behavior is transparent. They are acting big and trying to make others feel small to cover up their own insecurities. Healthy people see that, and find arm-farts during grown-up business meetings to be pathetic rather than funny.

Immature people also throw temper tantrums. Their emotional management skills are at a toddler's level of development. They routinely flip out over the most trivial matters. They become furious when larger problems arise, often lashing out at those who brought the issue to their attention. They are easily angered, and rage without constraint. This shows up as verbal abuse of others, slamming doors, throwing things, or a hundred other variations of childish behavior.

Immature people can also have adolescent style fits of rebelling and defying normal workplace protocols. Employees who are fixated on sexuality in an adolescent way are one example. They are the folks whose language is highly sexual in nature, and who twist just about anything that is said into having a sexual meaning. Another example is the employees who are deliberately loud and disruptive to their co-workers. They may refuse work assignments, slack off, whine, make excuses, and socialize rather than work. They take long breaks and lunches and expect everyone else to carry the load. They see work only as a paycheck, and are interested in doing the bare minimum necessary to keep it going. They treat professional workplaces like they are still at their first job at a fast food joint.

Notes _____

_____

_____

_____

_____

_____

_____

_____

_____

_____

_____

_____

_____

_____

_____

_____

_____

_____

_____

_____

_____

_____

_____

_____

_____

_____

_____

Section Two: Assess the Impact

After you have determined what the problem is, the next step is to assess the impact it is having on you. Healthy, productive workplaces help people grow into their best professional and personal selves. Their ripple impact is excellent, with the benefits of a happy workplace spilling over into their employee's relationships, family life, health, finances, and dreams outside the office. Everything is better because work is so good. Employees are able to relax, be well, and focus on the bigger picture of their life and what is important to them. They work hard, are rewarded for it, and enjoy the rest of their lives. Not enough workplaces in America today offer this kind of environment.

Bottom line, leadership isn't doing their job protecting their people, accomplishing the organizational mission, or adding value to the community. Very few organizations are in the middle, with a neutral impact on people and their lives. There are either good leaders creating good places to work, or bad leaders who are at the root of the problem environments. In their most severe form, chaotic, toxic, crazy making or other kinds of truly unhealthy work environments do a lot of damage to people, their lives, and their loved ones. Bad leaders eventually wear out even their very best employees. Vulnerable people are particularly hard hit by a bad leader's misdeeds. Everyone in the middle experiences different degrees of stress, frustration, and damage.

The Problem's Impact on You

Here is a list of ways bad leaders / bad workplaces can impact people. It is not an exhaustive list because negative environments and people affect each of us in different ways. Please mark the items that you are experiencing, or have experienced, so you can begin to get an accurate picture of the toll your work situation is taking on you:

- Feeling anxious
- Feeling depressed
- Feeling angry
- Feeling afraid
- Being short tempered
- Being stressed out
- Being seriously impatient
- Easily aggravated
- Trouble sleeping
- Physical health issues

- Physically worn out
- Mental health issues
- Emotionally worn out
- Loss of self-esteem
- Loss of self-confidence
- Loss of hope
- Loss of faith in other people
- Losing the ability to function
- Overwhelmed by daily life tasks
- Giving up important activities
- Financial problems
- Fear of the future
- Difficulty trusting other people
- Difficulty being around other people
- Tension with family or friends
- Others are worried about you
- Relationship / marriage problems
- Other change / problem not listed above:
- Other change / problem not listed above:
- Other change / problem not listed above:
- Other change / problem not listed above:
- Other change / problem not listed above:

YOUR IMPACT ON THE PROBLEM

Before we move on to figuring out how to minimize the impact, we need to take an honest look at whether or not we are contributing to making the problem worse. If we are impaired, have mental health issues, are engaged in criminal activities, are drama stagers, or if we are immature, there is no question we must address our own issues as part of the larger solution for the workplace. If that is your situation then you need to get help. Your workplace and your family will never be healthy or reach their potential if you have one of the issues listed above and aren't doing anything to fix it. It is your responsibility to address and resolve those issues. But even for those of us who are healthy and mature, it is important to make sure we are not inadvertently contributing to the issues. Here are several key questions to ask ourselves:

- Am I reacting rather than responding to what is happening around me?
- Are there instances in which I take the bait and end up in a negative situation I didn't instigate but didn't walk away from either?
- Am I harboring any ill intent towards anyone at my workplace?
- Am I locked in battle with anyone at work?
- Have I tried to take revenge against anyone?
- Have I deliberately slacked off because I am upset?

One of the best things we can do is learn to respond rather than react. There are a lot of good resources out there for learning the skills for doing this, but the most basic and effective thing we can do is simply pause. Pausing buys us time to regain control of our emotions and our brain's neurochemistry, and then we can think more clearly and decide how to handle the situation. We will almost always have a better outcome if we stop and consider options first.

Another key aspect of not making problems worse is developing the ability to become an observer of the environment, rather than a victim within it. This means that you stay one step back to more objectively see what is going on around you, rather than being right in the middle of the mess. This is a huge way to reclaim your own power rather than continuing to be at the mercy of people who do not have your best interest at heart. When you stay one step back, you can much more easily recognize people's motives and the root causes of the problems. You'll stop taking the bait when it is slung your way.

Another aspect of making sure you are part of the solution is not allowing yourself to harbor ill will, take revenge, or get locked into battle with anyone. These dynamics run in endless cycles and cause increasing damage along the way, especially to your own body, mind, and spirit. You already have to deal with enough stress hormones coursing through your body because of what is being done to you. Don't compound that damage by willingly allowing those kind of dark emotions and intentions to reside within you of your own accord. Acknowledge those feelings, then banish them and don't act on them. Finally, don't deliberately slack off, because all it does is hand your adversaries ammunition to use against you.

WHERE TO FIND HELP

Regardless of whether the problems you are having at work are caused by others, are of your own making, or both, there are time tested options for getting effective help. Only you know what will work for you, what you can afford, what fits with your personality, and what will work for your life as it stands right now. If you try one method and it isn't effective, that's ok. Move on to another one until you find something that helps. Here are several resources that have helped other people just like yourself reclaim their lives and move forward:

- 12 Step recovery groups
- Other types of structured recovery groups
- Creating a wellness plan with your physician
- Talking with a pastor or priest
- Attending church
- Counseling
- Spiritual direction
- Calling a suicide prevention hotline
- Finding a mentor
- Joining an accountability group
- Taking a vacation or leave of absence
- Doing career testing to explore new directions you might like to go
- Taking excellent care of yourself in body, mind, and spirit
- Starting a new hobby or sport, or joining a gym
- Making time for what matters to you outside of work
- Other:
- Other:
- Other:

ACTION PLAN TO MINIMIZE THE IMPACT

As painful as this realization is, intensely challenging situations give us the opportunity to grow in ways we otherwise might not have. It doesn't mean that we would choose them, or that we ignore the damage they are causing. It means shifting our perspective from feeling like we are stuck forever, to realizing that no matter how bad things are, we still have options and choices.

One of the most powerful choices we can make is to decide to become better not bitter. To choose to grow rather than give up or give in. When we walk into work each day committed to our own personal development, instead of waiting for the next bad thing to happen, it changes everything. The stress begins to fade away, and we feel better mentally and physically. The ripple effect on our life diminishes as we internalize less and less of the toxicity around us. This is not to say that we can ever perfectly resist the poison that others are trying to cram down our throats. It means that if we have a choice about whether or not to take that poison in, we don't do it. That one skill alone holds massive power to protect us.

One of the best things you can do when you are stuck in a toxic environment is to emotionally detach from the people and disinvest in the place. The best gift detachment offers us is that we start to see other people and their nonsense really, really clearly. What felt like (and no doubt was) a personal attack, now becomes merely a messed up person shouting into the wind. The power of people and places to hurt us when we practice detachment drops to an entirely tolerable degree. They are stripped of their ability to throw us off track, to wound us, to stop our progress. When we refuse to play the dysfunctional roles and follow the dysfunctional rules that have been forced upon us, we rediscover the gift of ourselves, our lives, and our dreams for the future. We are oppressed no longer. We rejoin the whole human race rather than obsessing about how things are going with the few jerks in our lives. We have the energy to play with our kids again, to love our partners again, to reengage in life again. We may take up an entirely new path or shift our lives in a far better direction.

Here are some key ways to take action to minimize the negative impact of toxic workplaces and create something positive in their place:

List skills you can develop to deal with the work issues on a daily basis:
-
-
-
-
-

List mental shifts you can make to gain a fresh perspective on your situation:
-
-
-
-
-

List ways you can detach and disinvest:

-
-
-
-
-

List things you can start doing to deal with the stress:

-
-
-
-
-

List things you can stop doing to avoid making the situation worse:

-
-
-
-
-

Describe activities you can start enjoying again, or new activities you'd like to try, to regain a sense of yourself outside of your workplace:

_____

_____

_____

_____

_____

_____

_____

_____

_____

_____

_____

SECTION THREE: STRATEGIES FOR MOVING FORWARD

After you have assessed the problem, its impact on you, and how to minimize the damage in the short-term, it is time to take a look at how to resolve the issue in the long-term. The best short-term strategies will eventually fail if the toxicity is so entrenched it permeates the environment, or if the chaos is relentless. Once you've got some short-term relief in place for yourself, you can think a lot more clearly about what you want your next step to be. Ultimately, you'll either be able to fix the problem itself to some degree, or you'll need to find ways to survive it when it can't be fixed.

SET A REALISTIC GOAL

There are four options for fixing what is wrong. It's important to take time to realistically assess the chances of each strategy being successful. It's also important to think through what the backlash of each strategy is likely to be. There are no guarantees, and only you can figure out what risks you are willing to take, and what costs you are willing to bear, in pursuit of a solution. You know the people, the system, and the issues better than anyone. Regaining your power starts with trusting your gut feelings and your thoughts about what might be effective.

Here are the options:

1. **Solve the problem in its entirety.** This means eradicating the problem for yourself, the team, the organization, and the community. Strategies include:

    a. Speaking directly with the problem individual to request or demand that the problem be resolved
    b. Reporting the problem to a trustworthy source
    c. Filing a complaint in-house
    d. Filing a complaint outside the organization
    e. Making a police report
    f. Requesting alternative dispute resolution
    g. Hiring an attorney
    h. Filing action in a formal adversarial process
    i. Going to an oversight body
    j. Going to Congress
    k. Going to the press

It may be more possible than you think to bring about change. It may also be more dangerous than you think. Especially in situations of corruption, you don't know how high up the chain or how widespread the network of people benefitting from the situation is. You may see just one small part of a much larger problem. However, if the problem is relatively local, even if it's a bad problem, you are much more likely to find someone who has the authority and the willingness to fix it. For example, if a manager for a local retail store is embezzling funds, but the national chain has a sterling reputation for honesty, you're probably going to find someone who cares about bringing the local manager back into line. But if the local manager is one of many across the country who are playing fast and loose with company funds, and the executives at the top of the chain are engaging in their own financial misdeeds, you are far less likely to find someone who cares and speaking up is only going to serve to make you a target. Perhaps you're ok with that and feel the need to speak up anyway. Some people do, sometimes with great results, sometimes with disastrous consequences.

The point is to try to trace the problem back to its origin. How did it get started? Who is involved? How big is the problem? Is it part of a system that tolerates or engages in wrongdoing? Or is it an anomaly in an otherwise excellent organization? The backlash for speaking up in a good organization is generally restricted to the problem individual being angry with you or trying to take action against you. Only they are losing the benefits of their misdeeds, and typically everyone else is happy to see the nonsense come to an end. But the backlash for speaking up in questionable or bad organizations, is a whole lot of people targeting you for as much damage as they can possibly inflict. If you're emotionally sturdy enough for the fight, then sometimes the fight is still worth it. Only you can decide, and those decisions should be made in consultation with your family. If you are in a leadership position you should also consult with the trusted members of your team. The consequences could very well impact them too.

2. **Influence the problem so that part of it is resolved.** This means significantly improving the problem for yourself, the team, the organization, and the community. Aspects of the problem will remain, but enough of it is fixed to allow a new and healthier chapter to begin. For example, if you have managers with multiple problems, you may not be able to resolve them all specifically, but you may be able to get someone to rein in the bad behavior generally. That kind of an outcome still greatly improves the environment for the team, and puts accountability in place where there was none before. The backlash is much more likely to come from just that one person, but because they are being watched,

they will only take it so far. Again, only you can determine if this is a wise option, and it should be done in consultation with your family, and if you are a leader, with the most trusted members of your team.

3. **Deal with the problem as it exists right now.** This means that you don't try to solve or influence the problem, and concentrate instead on finding ways to stop or minimize the impact it has on you. For example, if you realize that bad behavior is going on up and down the chain of command, and no one has any interest in acknowledging, let alone fixing the problem, you may decide that now is not the time to speak with any of the involved individuals or make any kind of report or complaint. Perhaps later, but not now. There's too much risk, the cost is too great, and your family and/or your team agrees it's a bad idea to take up the cause at the moment. If that is your situation, you are in fact stuck with dealing with the problem as it is.

   But as we talked about before, there is still a lot you can do to weather the storm with less damage. Detach, avoid making the problem worse, reengage with the rest of your life, take excellent care of yourself, and think about what you want your future to be like. On the toughest days, love your family and/or your team more than you hate your job. Get the support you need, and at the end of the bad day, just let it go. Let the emotions, the physical feelings, and your tired mind just dump all that stuff out and move on to the rest of your evening as best you can. Changing your own thinking, approach, or response will build an invaluable buffer zone in which you can find refuge. The backlash for this kind of strategy is minimal, because toxic people are rarely astute enough to recognize these kinds of subtle behavioral changes. You will be able to regain a lot of control over your own situation without them even realizing it. For the few that do realize it, their tactics will no longer work on you, and you'll still be much better off.

4. **Leave the situation because it is impossible to fix in any kind of timeframe that works for you.** This fixes the problem just for you, and that is entirely ok and legitimate because ultimately you can't save anyone else by sacrificing yourself. For example, if you've done all you can to resolve the issues, or decided there isn't anything that has a decent chance of success, and you've been hanging in there by coping with things as best you can but the place is still wearing you out in one way or another, it's time to either take a break or leave for good. Only you can decide if this is a feasible option. You can always take a vacation, call in sick, or take a leave of absence to get yourself some time and space to rest, relax, and think clearly about what you want to do. Maybe a break will

refresh you for a few weeks or months, or maybe even longer. But if there is no hope of positive change, and the impact is too negative to deal with, then in consultation with your family it's most likely time to come up with an exit plan. The backlash for leaving will only happen if you walk out too soon and place your family in financial jeopardy. Once you're free of the nonsense, you're free. You never have to see or interact with the problem people again, nor do you have to walk into a place that reeks of oppression and wasted potential. If you've secured another source of adequate income, your life gets right back on track and you will heal.

Notes _____

_____

_____

_____

_____

_____

_____

_____

_____

_____

_____

_____

_____

_____

_____

_____

_____

_____

_____

_____

_____

FINAL EXERCISE

To close out our time together, we're going to take everything we've learned today and put it into practice. What follows are three brief scenarios. I'd like you to make note of what you think the issues are and what you think is a good strategy for dealing with them. I'll give you a few minutes to do this, then we'll go over them as a group and close out the workshop.

SCENARIO #1: BUBBA JOE

Bubba Joe worked for a local outlet of a national retail store. He appointed himself king of the work environment. He didn't respect authority and was angry he wasn't chosen for a management position. Bubba Joe was lazy. He acted as the ringleader for a group of misfits who were also lazy and disruptive to the work environment. He declared himself the male role model, not just for the boys, but for everyone. He chased the ladies at work, and had been transferred around the country because of complaints about his behavior. He blamed his children for ruining his life because he wanted to spend his money on fancy cars and travel. He hated his wife, and spoke about her in highly derogatory terms.

He behaved in a loud, crude way most of the time. In meetings, he and his misfits sat in the back of the room and made fun of the speaker, the boss, and their peers. They made sure they were loud enough to be disruptive, and they showed off for each other by seeing who could come up with the best insult or argument to upset whoever was speaking at the time. Both men and women complained about Bubba Joe's behavior, and several great employees had left the organization because of him. In their exit interviews, they candidly stated that Bubba Joe was the reason for their departure. They also urged the company to do something about him before any kind of an incident broke out between him and another employee.

Bubba Joe had a temper, and would rage, slamming doors, throwing pens, and yelling at people. He was a bully and would get in people's faces and shout at them. His goal was to provoke a physical altercation. Several employees had come close to taking that bait. His behavior was totally out of control, and made people feel threatened and afraid. Bubba Joe enjoyed causing people this kind of distress.

In addition to dominating the work environment, his goal was also to hook up with one of the ladies at work. He would sidle up to them, talk about how his wife wasn't treating him right, then pull them in close to him and try to steer them to his office. Several women had complained about this behavior, but because it was not technically considered to be sexual contact, nothing was ever done. Everyone knew that it was only a matter of time before Bubba Joe crossed the sexual line with someone, but management always seemed to take his side. Bubba Joe was obsessed with sex. He spoke frequently about his weekend conquests, could turn even the most neutral conversations into sexual ones, and frequently made obscene gestures in the work environment. This was the type of behavior that had gotten him moved from place to place.

Furthermore, Bubba Joe had a history of run-ins with the law stretching all the way back to his teenage years. He graduated from high school only due to special accommodations he had been given for his behavioral issues. He never served in the military, and drifted from entry level job to entry level job for years. He was hired into his current job only because one of his relatives worked for the company. He planned to stay with the company until retirement, which was still many years away. The new local manager was quite taken with Bubba Joe, and found his behavior to be charming. She had been on the job for less than a month, having been transferred in from another part of the country. She had a sleazy reputation, and had formal complaints filed against her at every one of her previous stores. She had also gotten her job through a relative who had risen to the executive level, and sometimes the two of them turned business trips into vacations, using the company credit card to finance their adventures. Inevitably, these jaunts were discovered on the company's credit card statement. The home office made the executive pay it back but otherwise did not discipline her. They also kept it quiet from the Board of Directors, who as far as anyone could tell, was unaware of any of the problems going on within the company.

Where do the issues lie:
- Co-worker
  - Why or why not?
- Leader
  - Why or why not?
- System
  - Why or why not?

What are the issues:
- Addiction
  - Why or why not?
- Mental health
  - Why or why not?

- Criminal activity
  - Why or why not?
- Drama staging
  - Why or why not?
- Immaturity
  - Why or why not?

What strategies have a good chance of being successful:
- Solving the problem in its entirety
  - Why or why not?
- Influence the problem so part of it is resolved
  - Why or why not?
- Deal with the problem as it is now
  - Why or why not?
- Leave the situation because the problem is impossible to fix
  - Why or why not?

Other thoughts:

_____

_____

_____

_____

_____

_____

_____

_____

_____

_____

_____

_____

_____

_____

_____

SCENARIO #2: RUTHIE

Ruthie's mama was a drug addict. Ruthie followed in her footsteps and began drinking heavily in high school. Somehow she managed to function well enough to graduate, go on to college, and land a decent corporate job. The organization was huge, with global outposts all over the world. The corporation enjoyed a sterling reputation and prided itself on honest business practices, treating employees well, and giving back to each community of which they were a part. Employees were given time off one day per quarter to volunteer, and for every ten years they were with the company, they could choose a location anywhere in the world to volunteer for two weeks, all expenses paid. The managers in the organization were carefully selected, and went through monthly training to help them build increasingly advanced skills. Morale was excellent, business was booming, and profits were at an all-time high.

Ruthie had managed to hide her drinking well enough to pass the rigorous interviews for the management training program. She had been with the company for a year, and so far, had gotten along well with her co-workers and supervisors alike. She had aspired to the management program, and had carefully guarded her secret. She had been managing well enough, making friends, getting good reviews about her performance, and building a reputation as a team player. But it didn't take long before the pressure of the management job began to get to Ruthie. Her carefully concealed world began to crumble. When she went out with her work friends she still managed to keep her drinking under control. But at home, she began drinking much more than she had been before. She started showing up for work hungover. At first it was a running joke, there were a lot of people who occasionally overdid it and showed up on Monday still under the weather. But for Ruthie, those Mondays turned into Tuesdays, and then Wednesdays, and so on until it seemed she was showing up hungover more often than not. People were beginning to notice, but she was still treating people well, so she had a lot of forgiveness that was readily granted to her. She managed to be productive, which kept her issues from appearing on the radar screen of the higher ups.

The increased drinking didn't help Ruthie's stress. In fact it made it worse. She began to feel bad about herself, realizing she was headed down the same path as her mother. This terrified her, but she had been drinking for so long she had no idea how to stop. She had kept her secret so well for so many years, there wasn't anyone in her life she could talk to honestly about what was going on. She made a private vow to get herself back together. But as she progressed through the training program, she was given increasing responsibility. She began to crack under the pressure. Her adult life had been so carefully arranged. She was able to drink and still do the things she wanted to do. She deliberately kept the stress level in her life as low as possible, to be able to keep functioning well and keep her secret hidden. But she had really wanted the management position. She really liked the idea of leading and helping others.

She wanted a much more stable life than her mother had provided for her, and a promotion would go a long way towards building that foundation. She dreamed of a husband, children, home ownership, and happy family vacations at the beach. She was well educated, talented, and wanted to make a difference in the world. But she had never learned how to deal with her stress, except to drink. That had been her example. As the months went by, even the extra drinking at home wasn't helping. The hangovers had eased up considerably as her body adjusted to the increased amounts of alcohol, and people were no longer noticing or making comments about it. In fact unbeknownst to them, she had brought in a small supply of alcohol just a couple of weeks prior, in case she needed it during the day. She knew this was a bad decision to make, but so far she hadn't gotten caught.

But on one fateful day, she had just gotten out of a management meeting where a new company initiative was announced. She would be working closely with a high level group of senior managers. Ruthie knew the gig was up, and she was either going to have to get her drinking under control or she could lose everything she had worked so hard to build. She knew that the executive team prided itself on being healthy, mature, professional individuals. Their efforts to make the world a better place extended even beyond the work environment. They would get together several times a year to conduct visioning, strategic planning, and teambuilding exercises for carefully vetted non-profits in the community. As a team they were a formidable force for good. Their relentless compassion and enthusiasm were the stuff of legend.

The workforce greatly admired the executives and was inspired by them. Everyone felt blessed because they realized what a rare organization they worked for. Sure they had their occasional skirmishes and problems to sort out, but even then the issues were handled in a caring way that both solved things and strengthened relationships. Ruthie was simultaneously in awe of the executives and terrified of them. She went back to her office to have a drink to calm her nerves, because she was on the verge of complete panic about what would happen when her secret was inevitably found out. She didn't have to wonder long, because two of her employees excitedly entered her office to share their project results. They stopped in their tracks and stared at the open vodka bottle on Ruthie's desk. A heavy silence suddenly hung in the air.

Where do the issues lie:
- Co-worker
  - Why or why not?
- Leader
  - Why or why not?
- System
  - Why or why not?

What are the issues:

- Addiction
  - Why or why not?
- Mental health
  - Why or why not?
- Criminal activity
  - Why or why not?
- Drama staging
  - Why or why not?
- Immaturity
  - Why or why not?

What can Ruthie do to help herself?

- 12 Step recovery groups
- Other types of structured recovery groups
- Creating a wellness plan with her physician
- Talking with a pastor or priest
- Attending church
- Counseling
- Spiritual direction
- Calling a suicide prevention hotline
- Finding a mentor
- Joining an accountability group
- Taking a vacation or leave of absence
- Doing career testing to explore new directions she might like to go
- Taking excellent care of herself in body, mind, and spirit
- Starting a new hobby or sport, or joining a gym
- Making time for what matters to her outside of work
- Other:
- Other:
- Other:

What strategies have a good chance of being successful:

- Solving the problem in its entirety
  - Why or why not?

- Influence the problem so part of it is resolved
  - Why or why not?
- Deal with the problem as it is now
  - Why or why not?
- Leave the situation because the problem is impossible to fix
  - Why or why not?

Other thoughts:

_____

_____

_____

_____

_____

_____

_____

_____

_____

_____

_____

_____

_____

_____

_____

_____

_____

_____

_____

_____

_____

_____

_____

SCENARIO #3: JEZEBEL

Jezebel considered herself to be one of the smartest people alive. She engaged in a lot of subtle put downs of those around her. She treated her co-workers the same as she treated her family, with disdain and contempt. But she hid her feelings behind a fake smile and artificial laugh, both of which were designed to disarm the person she was speaking to. She had a need to be the center of attention, and quickly turned any conversation towards being about her. She bragged about her accomplishments, her importance, and her extraordinary plans for the future.

Historically, she had a series of best friends whom she would immerse herself with to a point that began making people uncomfortable. These were always people she felt could benefit her in some way. She would elicit their sympathy for her plight in life, which always carried a theme of being a victim. Anyone who dared suggest that such a lengthy history of difficulty might be at least partly her responsibility, was immediately cast out of her world. She would follow that up with as much social violence as she possibly could, trash talking the individual far and wide. She was able to bamboozle several best friends to rescue her from the boogeymen she constantly perceived in her environment. But once those friends had served her purpose, she discarded them mercilessly. If she noticed one of her castaways becoming friends with someone else, she would pit one against the other, sometimes making up complete lies to cause problems between them.

If someone received some kind of recognition, she would publicly vilify that person and try to damage their reputation. People who used to be her friends were sometimes embarrassed they had not seen the game for what it was. They were also afraid of her, which she delighted in. She made sure everyone knew that she held great power to cause them trouble, even though she had never held a management position. In fact she had been quietly relocated from department to department because of her odd and troubling behavior. Yet she told everyone that she had been hand picked by the President of the company to monitor quality control across the organization.

She let everyone know that it was only a matter of time before the executives would select her to join their ranks, even though the actual process was highly competitive and arduous. She always made a grand entrance to meetings, swooping in vastly overdressed. She acted as though she was sure this would be the meeting in which her promotion to a high level position would be announced. Once the meeting was underway and it was clear it was about routine matters, she would abruptly leave, typically causing some kind of disruption on her way out the door. When her best friend of the week would go to lunch with her, she was rude to the wait staff and had gotten into more than one verbal altercation with fellow diners. It seemed that everywhere she went she caused confusion and upset where there had been none before.

Where do the issues lie:

- Co-worker
  - Why or why not?
- Leader
  - Why or why not?
- System
  - Why or why not?

What are the issues:

- Addiction
  - Why or why not?
- Mental health
  - Why or why not?
- Criminal activity
  - Why or why not?
- Drama staging
  - Why or why not?
- Immaturity
  - Why or why not?

What strategies have a good chance of being successful:

- Solving the problem in its entirety
  - Why or why not?
- Influence the problem so part of it is resolved
  - Why or why not?
- Deal with the problem as it is now
  - Why or why not?
- Leave the situation because the problem is impossible to fix
  - Why or why not?

Other thoughts:

_____

_____

_____

_____

_____

ANSWER KEY TO SCENARIO BASED EXERCISES

SCENARIO #1: BUBBA JOE

Where do the issues lie:

- Co-worker - Yes
  - Why or why not?
    - Bubba Joe clearly has multiple issues, which we will detail below. He is instigating a lot of conflict without any precipitating factors from anyone else.
- Leader - Yes
  - Why or why not?
    - New local leader is charmed by his behavior.
    - None of the leaders above Bubba Joe have ever held him accountable.
- System - Yes
  - Why or why not?
    - The common practice in this organization is to move people around rather than discipline them.
    - Complaints about Bubba Joe are never taken seriously.
    - Good people keep leaving the organization and citing him as the reason in their exit interviews.
    - Company has never acted on the repeated warnings they received about his volatile behavior.
    - He is allowed to repeatedly disrupt the workplace without consequence.
    - His touching and grabbing of female employees was classified as non-sexual.
    - He is allowed to continually make sexual comments in the workplace.
    - The financial misdeeds of the executive were not disciplined.
    - Company problems are concealed from the Board of Directors.

What are the issues:

- Addiction - Not based on information presented
  - Why or why not?
    - No mention or suggestion of addiction issues at present or in Bubba Joe's past.
- Mental health - Not based on information presented   ▪ Why or why not?
    - No mention or suggestion of mental health issues at present or in Bubba Joe's past.
- Criminal activity - Yes

- Why or why not?
    - History of run-ins with the law stretching back to when he was a teenager. There aren't any details given, but we know it is a long-standing problem.
  - Drama staging - Yes
    - Why or why not?
      - Appointed himself king over everyone else.
      - Manipulates people and engineers situations to act out his need to dominate people, places, and things.
      - He is a ringleader of a group of misfits that bully and harass their co-workers.
  - Immaturity - Yes
    - Why or why not?
      - Blames his family for depriving him of a lifestyle free of responsibility.
      - Temper tantrums.
      - Sexual acting out in the work environment.

What strategies have a good chance of being successful:
  - Solving the problem in its entirety - Not likely
    - Why or why not?
      - Problems run rampant and are covered up.
      - Disconnect between management and the Board of Directors.
      - Individuals moved around rather than held accountable.
      - Issues are systemic, at all levels of the organization, across the entire country.
  - Influence the problem so part of it is resolved - Possibly
    - Why or why not?
      - It would take a lot of careful effort and a significant amount of risk to find someone who cared enough to intervene, who also had the power to fix the problems.
  - Deal with the problem as it is now - Absolutely
    - Why or why not?
      - Excellent self-care, detachment, and disinvestment would go a long way towards mitigating the impact Bubba Joe's behavior had on the individual. There is also support from the other good workers being affected by his nonsense.
      - He also has a history of pushing things too far and being moved, so it would make sense to hold out hope that he will be moved again.

- Bubba Joe's targets could also confront him directly about his behavior. Since no one is held accountable anyway, there probably wouldn't be any consequences for standing up to him and telling him to knock it off.
- Police intervention might be a possibility if he continues to grab/grope people. If the company is unwilling to do anything, the law might, especially since Bubba Joe has had police involvement before.

- Leave the situation because the problem is impossible to fix - If necessary
  - Why or why not?
    - Other people have left because of Bubba Joe's behavior, but we don't know what strategies they tried for dealing with it. Perhaps someone will use a better strategy that will be more effective.
    - However, it also remains true that life is short and if Bubba Joe is creating intolerable problems, each person must decide for themselves if/when it is time to go.

Other thoughts:
  - Bubba Joe's problems are pervasive across environments, including work, home, and out in the community. He has rigid patterns of behavior that are both immature and drama staging. Unless there is a life-altering event that takes place, the likelihood of Bubba Joe choosing to change is right about zero.
  - Many organizations run scared of the Bubba Joes and allow them to run roughshod over the team and poison the environment. Because Bubba Joe has never been held accountable, there is no hope for resolution from above. Weak leaders will at best simply pass him along so he can be someone else's problem.
  - One aspect of good news in the scenario is that Bubba Joe already has been turned down for a promotion, which means there is some recognition of his issues. He may not be held accountable for them, but he also will not be given more power to create even bigger problems.
  - Another good possibility is that the new local manager will continue getting herself in trouble as well. If she is transferred out and a healthy, strong local manager is transferred in, then the entire work environment could be saved. Someone brave enough to rein in Bubba Joe's behavior would transform the work environment very quickly. When problems are entrenched over the long-term, people welcome even incremental change in a positive direction.
  - Going to the Board of Directors would be a possibility, but it is unknown what kind of relationships or motivations may exist. The Board would either be properly horrified and intervene, or they would help hide the problems if it meant a buddy might get in trouble.

Scenario #2: Ruthie

Where do the issues lie:

- Co-worker - Yes
  - Why or why not?
    - Ruthie's drinking is causing the problem. It is not even partially to blame on anyone else, including her mother. Ruthie has lost control of her drinking. Everything she holds dear, as well as her future prospects, is in jeopardy.
- Leader - No
  - Why or why not?
    - Ruthie's leaders are completely unaware of her drinking.
- System - No
  - Why or why not?
    - From the description, this is a robustly healthy and productive workplace. There are no known problems, or problem individuals that are causing an adverse impact. Accountability and growth are key aspects of the environment as well as the people within it, especially the executive team.

What are the issues:

- Addiction - Yes
  - Why or why not?
    - Ruthie grew up in addicted household.
    - She is an alcoholic. Her life revolves around her drinking, she has developed tolerance, and she continues to take risks she would normally never even consider, let alone act on.
- Mental health - Not based on information presented
  - Why or why not?
    - No mention or suggestion of mental health issues at present or in Ruthie's past.
- Criminal activity - Not based on information presented
  - Why or why not?
    - No mention or suggestion of criminal activity at present or in Ruthie's past.
- Drama staging - No
  - Why or why not?
    - Ruthie is desperately attempting to perform her job well, and forge good working relationships with other people.

- She is well-liked by a cross section of people, and seen as a team player.
- She has not had any interpersonal battles with anyone.
- With the exception of the alcohol, she focuses on work while at work.
- She does not have any hidden agendas, nor does she demonstrate ill-will towards anyone.
  - Immaturity - No
    - Why or why not?
      - Ruthie does not act up or act out. With the exception of the alcohol, she behaves as a mature professional who is taking her career seriously.
      - She treats people well, even despite her drinking.

What can Ruthie do to help herself?
- Go to inpatient treatment
- Go to outpatient treatment
- Join a 12 Step recovery group
- Join a different type of structured recovery group
- Find a sponsor or a mentor
- Talk with a pastor or a priest
- Go to counseling
- Other:
- Other:
- Other:

What strategies have a good chance of being successful:
- Solving the problem in its entirety - Excellent chance
  - Why or why not?
    - Ruthie is no longer alone. Her secret is out and the healing can begin. There is no question that the company does not know about her problem, and that they would want to know.
    - Problems in Ruthie's organization are handled so that the issue gets resolved and the relationships are strengthened. There are no witch hunts, public shaming, or quick firings that take place.
    - The executive team, whom Ruthie is now closely associated with, is renowned throughout the company and the community for their compassion. They have a demonstrated heart for helping people heal, so there is very little question they will treat Ruthie and her problem in the same way.

- Influence the problem so part of it is resolved - Not necessary
  - Why or why not?
    - Once the leadership learns about Ruthie's issue, she will no doubt be given their full support to make a full recovery.
- Deal with the problem as it is now - Not necessary
  - Why or why not?
    - Ruthie's behavior has not caused anyone at the company any trouble.
    - The employees who caught her drinking can be given support as well, and the executives can make efforts to repair any damage that was done because of this incident. It is entirely possible that Ruthie and her staff will be grateful they walked in on her, so that she could finally get help.
- Leave the situation because the problem is impossible to fix - Not necessary
  - Why or why not?
    - Again, Ruthie has not harmed anyone else except for the isolated incident of causing embarrassment and concern. Her track record is so good that what happened can be accurately categorized as one problem that needs to be resolved.

Other thoughts:

- Ruthie is one of those rare people who is in fact good enough the vast majority of the time. This is why asking the #1 question is so critically important. She is a great leader who made a bad mistake, who has a real and serious problem. She is not a leader who is a jerk most of the time, likes to inflict damage, or in other ways has proven herself to be untrustworthy. She deserves a chance to overcome her problem and go on to be a big success.
- The employees in this story have a couple of options. They can encourage Ruthie to step forward on her own and get help, or they can go to leadership themselves. Either way, it is imperative that the information comes out so Ruthie can start the recovery process. Covering up for her will result in harm being done and Ruthie starting down a destructive path.
- This story is a great example of how even good leaders are still human, and can have issues they need to work through. It does not mean all is lost, just that a lot of hard work needs to be done to move forward in a positive direction.
- It is possible that other people in the organization, including those on the executive team, may be in recovery as well. We all have baggage to work through, and in a large organization it is likely that at least someone else has faced and triumphed over addiction.

Ruthie may end up with a strong in-house support network that will walk with her every step of the way.

- With the secrecy behind her, Ruthie has the opportunity to make new choices and create a future of meaning and happiness for herself. As she works to break the bonds of addiction, a whole new world of possibilities and opportunities opens up to her. She gets to choose how she wants to live, rather than remaining ensnared in generational patterns of behavior that no longer serve her.

SCENARIO #3: JEZEBEL

Where do the issues lie:
- Co-worker - Yes
  - Why or why not?
    - Jezebel is instigating all kinds of trouble at the workplace. Any chaos going on around her can be traced right back to her.
- Leader - Yes, partially
  - Why or why not?
    - There is an acknowledgement that her behavior is strange and problematic.
    - However, the response has been to quietly keep moving her around, rather than hold her accountable.
- System - Yes, partially
  - Why or why not?
    - It is unclear whether or not the key decision makers in the organization are aware of Jezebel's issues.
    - We do not know if Jezebel's situation is unusual, or if the status quo in the organization is to move problems around rather than solve them.
    - We can tell that the leaders are getting permission from someone to transfer Jezebel, rather than make her responsible for her actions.

What are the issues:
- Addiction - Not based on information presented
  - Why or why not?
    - No mention or suggestion of addiction issues at present or in Jezebel's past.

- ○ Mental health - Not based on information presented
  - ▪ Why or why not?
    - • No mention or suggestion of mental health issues at present or in Jezebel's past.
- ○ Criminal activity - Not based on information presented
  - ▪ Why or why not?
    - • No mention or suggestion of criminal activity at present or in Jezebel's past.
- ○ Drama staging - Yes
  - ▪ Why or why not?
    - • Jezebel has a rigid and pervasive view of herself as better than everyone else. This includes her colleagues, her family, and members of the community.
    - • She is committing premeditated social violence every chance she gets.
    - • She enjoys causing other people pain.
    - • She is a star in her own story, and assigns others roles that suit her. When they have outlived their usefulness to her, she casts them away like an outdated costume.
    - • She vacillates between sweeping charming behaviors, to despondent "save me" type pleas.
    - • She is possessive and pits people against each other.
    - • She deliberately lies about people.
    - • She viciously fights facing reality. Despite being in serious trouble for her transgressions, and never having held a leadership position, she believes that she was specially appointed to oversee the work of others. If anyone tries to point out the problems she is causing, she ferociously attacks them.
- ○ Immaturity - Yes
  - ▪ Why or why not?
    - • Even though there are not many details in the story to indicate specific examples of this, we do know that drama stagers by definition cannot or will not handle healthy adult roles and responsibilities. Jezebel is stuck in an earlier stage of development, including magical thinking, unreasonable demands, and a refusal to follow the rules.

What strategies have a good chance of being successful:
- ○ Solving the problem in its entirety - Not likely
  - ▪ Why or why not?
    - • Jezebel has been moved around rather than held accountable

- Influence the problem so part of it is resolved - Possibly
  - Why or why not?
    - If the current people she is tormenting speak up, it might be possible to get her moved again.
- Deal with the problem as it is now - Absolutely
  - Why or why not?
    - Detachment and disinvestment from having anything to do with Jezebel will neutralize a great deal of her impact. There is no question she will cycle through people. Once someone has been cast aside, their turn is over for the most part. She may try to continue to cause them problems, but once they see behind her mask, she knows they will never be under her control again. She will move on to someone else she perceives as susceptible to her manipulation.
    - There will be a growing cadre of people who have also seen behind the mask, who will support each other. Once the truth is seen for what it is, relationships will often mend.
    - Excellent self-care can offset the personal damage that was done.
    - As she continues to create the same problems everywhere she is moved, it becomes harder for her to continue to hide behind the mask. As the truth is revealed, her ability to inflict career damage is greatly reduced.
- Leave the situation because the problem is impossible to fix - If necessary
  - Why or why not?
    - If Jezebel for some reason refuses to let go of a target and relentlessly preys upon that person, it can become a much more serious situation. She may escalate and start invading the person's life outside of work. If that is the case, there may even be an element of danger. If complaining is too risky, or if the situation is not taken seriously, then it may very well be time to leave.

Other thoughts:
- Any Jezebel is an unmitigated disaster in the work environment. They can take any formerly functioning environment and throw it into total chaos. If your team was doing alright before and suddenly there is a great deal of confusion and conflict, look closely to see if there is a Jezebel right in the middle of it.
- They do not see that they are the common denominator in the problems they experience in every aspect of their life.
- They have a very limited emotional range, and often misperceive what someone else is actually feeling. Their primary emotion is anger, so they see anger just about everywhere,

and often where it is not. They are extremely reactive to what they perceive as other people's emotions, rather than having empathy for what the other person's emotions actually are.

- o They vigilantly scan for any challenge to their narrative, and fight it as if it is a matter of life and death. They perceive personal attacks where there are none.
- o They have a great deal of internal strife, and look for outside reasons to blame it on. They will suddenly pick fights just to relieve their inner tension. They are generally seen as hostile, cold, or unstable.

CONCLUSION

It's been an honor to share this time with you. I hope this resource has provided you with some new tools for dealing with really tough work situations. Don't ever give up. Keep fighting until you find something effective that helps you get your life back. You can make a difference, if not for your team or your organization, then at least for yourself and your family. Everyone deserves a safe, healthy, productive place to work. I admire your bravery in taking on the challenge, and I wish you well as you seek to be a difference maker.

Respectfully yours,
Deb

© *Annie Rubens*

www.debhollandlcsw.com

Publication Information

Taming the Toxic Workplace © 2016 by Deb Holland. All rights reserved. No part of this book may be used or reproduced in any manner whatsoever, including Internet usage, without written permission from the author, except in case of brief quotations embodied in reviews.

First Edition
First Printing, 2016

Library of Congress Cataloging-in-Publication Data
Holland, Deb
Taming the Toxic Workplace / Deb Holland - 1st ed.
Library of Congress Control Number: 2016905691
CreateSpace Independent Publishing Platform, North Charleston, SC
ISBN 13: 978-1530498963
ISBN 10: 1530498963
1) Toxic workplace, 2) Difficult people, 3) Bad boss, 4) Hate job, 5) Conflict resolution

Disclaimer
All characters appearing in this work are fictitious. Any resemblance to real people, living or dead, is entirely coincidental. All locations / settings are also fictitious. Teaching points and story examples are fictionalized, composite representations of the experiences I've had over the course of my working life. None of them depict any specific individual or organization at any time in my working history.

Photographs © Annie Rubens, used with permission

Workbook design by Fran Schiesl, Spot-on-Graphics